YOU ARE YOUR OUTCOME

Don't bury your setbacks in misery, take action today and you won't have to suffer tomorrow.

"INSTEAD OF AVOIDING CHALLENGES, PERHAPS WE SHOULD EMBRACE THE FACT LIFE'S ONLY TRAINING US FOR WHAT WE'RE ASKING FOR." -TERRENCE SANI

TERRENCESANI
SPEAKER · COACH · LIFE CHANGER

Terrence is a true advocate who speaks the importance of discovering who you truly are and associating yourself with your life's purpose.

Book Terrence for your next event!
1 (832) -943 - GAIN (4246)
HELLO@TERRENCESANI.COM
TERRENCESANI.COM

What if I told you, everything you're __comfortable__ doing is the reason why you aren't where you want to be?

If you can digest change, you can output results.

"You Are Your Outcome is a reminder of how we often take the daily things in our life for granted and that not everyone's business is our business."
-Darlene J.

"I would recommend this book to young entrepreneurs or ambitious individuals looking to excel in their careers. Learning your true strengths and weaknesses within yourself is essential on your road to success!"
-Hillary W.

Stop giving obstacles the tools to build a lifestyle you don't want.

YOU ARE YOUR OUTCOME

HOW TO ELIMINATE SELF MADE OBSTACLES, SETBACKS AND FEAR

TERRENCE SANI

Thank You

I want to thank and congratulate you for purchasing this book.

Honestly, I've had some resistance with the title. I've even been told the phrase "you are your outcome" is offensive. People don't often ever enjoy the finger being pointed at them. Well, there's good news. I'm not going to point the finger at you either, nor will I attempt to hold your hand.

What I need is for you to point the finger at yourself!

It's easy to take a win, but taking a loss builds character. When things go right everyone's all in, but the moment situations get heated people drop integrity like it's hot.

This book contains digestible steps, strategies and concepts I've personally obtained through the years on how to bulldoze common self-made obstacles and setbacks that stop you from getting the outcome you desire.

It doesn't matter if you're first in line to any opportunity. Because, if you don't have the key to open the door it's as if you were never present.

I've spent over 20 years coasting, letting life and the people in it dictate my path and purpose. Oh but now.. now it's time to grab life by the back of the head and show the world who's boss!

I'm an only child, I had to fire my siblings:

Shoulda, woulda and coulda.

THIS BOOK IS DEDICATED TO:

Anyone who refuses to forfeit their self-expression for tolerable discomfort, stability and financial gain.

A true **Freethinker**.

The tools for success are hidden in action.

YOUR ONSLAUGHT TO VICTORY

14 | ACKNOWLEDGEMENTS

16 | MY AWAKENING
My wake up moment and outcome

26 | YOU vs OPTIMISM
Devil's advocate, thoughts & action

36 | YOU vs FAILURE
Getting to know yourself, doubting yourself,
programming & conditioning and death

50 | YOU vs BAD HABITS
Forming habits, unproductive habits,
paralyzed analysis, avoiding a rut, pride, help
& lifelines

56 | YOU vs CONTRIBUTION
Venting, growing seeds, becoming belittled
and backdoored, what's your outlet?

64 | YOU vs SETBACKS
Are you a quitter?, your B.S. dilemma, seeing
your future

74 | YOU vs SELF

78 | YOU vs CONSCIOUSNESS

Direct deposit happy, backup plans, seize the moment, pay attention

88 | YOU vs DEAD WEIGHT

Procrastination isn't a disease, bridging the gap

94 | YOU vs HUSTLE

Embrace the hustle, how to hustle, advantage of hustling

100 | YOU vs SECURITY

Stop suffering, structure, degrees aren't guarantees

Top level anything needs bottom level everything.

I truly believe I was born for a purpose and not on purpose.

ACKNOWLEDGEMENTS

I'd like to thank my mother Karen for teaching me to be open-minded and to always look at situations from more than one angle.

My wife Ashley for the many sacrifices you've made, showing me what true love is and believing in me throughout my trials and tribulations.

Carl for teaching me the value of laughter.

My dad for teaching me sometimes the people you care about the most, will be attracted to negativity and dismiss opportunity.

My kids Hezekiah, Hendrix and baby Norah for giving me a reason to wake up and take care of business.

The 5th Quarter Living Movement, Eric Thomas Breathe University Family, Sleepless Knights, Texas Trotters Toastmasters, any past, current and future mentors that provide value.

Tony for giving me your laptop when my car got broken into and telling me to keep going.

Mrs. Butler for writing me up because I refused to do my homework in class and then reporting it to my Orchestra teacher. You taught me how people can go the extra mile for foolishness.

Mrs. Wallace-Carbon for firing me while my wife was pregnant. You've shown me how playing it safe is a subpar chess move.

Why are we so afraid to do everything it takes to get what we want and so comfortable doing everything that holds us back?

My Awakening

I majored in procrastination, pink slips (both termination and late notice letters), pushing priorities to the limit and stretching deadlines out as much as possible. I even took my time getting out of the womb, my birthday is the last day of the year December 31st. The day all things end and expire. Like coupons, sales, milk etc.

But when it all comes down to it I don't take it personally, the entire world celebrates my birthday. But to be fully honest, the world also participates in a yearly countdown for New Year's Eve to end. Believe it or not, ironically my grandmother was born January first of all days.

Growing up my mom a Christian who worked both day and night but somehow in some super mom fashion was always there for me. If needed I had access to my father, a Muslim born and raised in Nigeria who had come here to America to go to school. Even though my parents never lived together, he convinced me to change my last name from Hunter which was my mom's last name to Sani.

I was told son's in Africa always bare their father's last name. Originally, I hated the idea but went with it out of pity. Nowadays I pride myself on carrying his name. "Sani" in Hausa an African dialect means "to know" or "brilliant".

Mom once said after having me she didn't want any more children. I wasn't a bad child but there was one time when I was two, mom poured a cup of cold water on me because I was acting up in K-Mart. Another time I bit her on the hand inside of a Pistol Pete's Pizza, for not having enough tickets for the prize I wanted. Which was nothing but a super fancy mechanical pencil. She still has that scar to this day.

While most moms would have gone upside my head and made an example out of this experience. Mom never once raised a hand towards me, why? Because, whenever she was really upset she would look at me and squint her eyes in anger.

Even though it sounds dumb now, back then it would literally make me cry so hard that my throat would lock up when trying to talk. Why is it that parents always wanna ask questions when you can't talk correctly? Having not ever felt the raft of the "leather fury" led me to forever live in fear of the unknown.

That was until she became the legal guardian of my two older cousins Cedrick and Lakisha. She'd actually whip them! Never in front of me, but seeing their faces afterward quickly taught me what not to do.

But, if anything did go wrong my grandmother Elizabeth who also helped raise me always had my back and took up for me. Like many African American grandmothers, mine was really religious. One Saturday morning I was eating her breakfast special: Scrambled eggs, white rice with butter and sugar, two biscuits with butter and grape jelly and lastly a cup of milk in my special yellow cup.

This particular Saturday morning while I was sitting at the edge of the bed watching X-Men, I mentioned how the character "Storm" was fighting evil and grandma responded with "Now you know Terrence, don't nobody control the weather but the lawd".

As I would grow older into my teens, both my cousins had left school on their own terms to live their own lives. Music and martial arts were the only major outlets I had. During my sophomore year of high school, my grandmother had lost an ongoing battle with breast cancer. During the funeral, my father arrived but sat in the back and later gave my mother a handshake. That's when I realized nobody will show me how to be a man but life.

I didn't sell drugs but saw the effects of how it affected my family enough to not want anything to do with it, ever. There were a few late nights my uncle would come home at two or three in the morning smelling like alcohol with a swollen eye, busted nose and lip after he'd been mugged. After seeing this a few times I guess you could say I was scared straight.

I wasn't ever in trouble with the law. The first time I tried skipping school I left with my best friend Cory, we got caught by a police officer and were told we'd get a ticket for truancy if caught again. I was an African American cellist with ethnically diverse friends. But ironically I didn't stand out, I just fit in.

I attended Alief Elsik High School. The greatest challenge I had was math. If you mix numbers with letters you will lose me every time guaranteed. I developed a bad habit, a motto actually. "It's better to cheat than to repeat".

That little mantra would be my handicap for all things academic. Little did I know it was a hidden concoction for a catastrophic disaster. I turned cheating into a sport, never wanting to get caught forced me to come up with new refreshing ideas. I even went out on a limb to borrow my friend's compact makeup and mirror set so that I had a small compartment to put my answers or notes and a mirror to see if the teacher was coming.

The second semester of my senior year of high school my mother had met a man Mr. Carl aka "Fri-dog" who would eventually become my stepfather. Mom slowly started coming home late, giving me money here and there. Till eventually those late nights just became check-in phone calls.

Let me paint the picture for you, I was a senior with a four bedroom two story townhouse all to myself and a revolving door of friends and parties. You couldn't tell me anything. Well, you could but it would surely go in one ear and out the other.

My grades in Spanish were so bad that in order to graduate I had to change my whole entire academic program to what's known as the "minimum plan" basically allowing me to graduate on time as long as I met the minimum credit requirements for the state of Texas.

This allowed me to drop courses I didn't need and enroll in remedial courses which caused gaps in my schedule. In my final semester, the algebra teacher was so concerned about cheating that there were three different formats of the test. Unable to acquire the answer log in time to copy all the answers, I was forced to actually take the test without a handicap.

I didn't know I was going to pass the twelfth grade and graduate until two days before it all went down. This means, the entire time I was taking senior pictures, sending out invitations and ordering my cap and gown, I was driving a train entirely on uncertainty and faith. Which was hands down one of the scariest moments of my life. With over 700 graduating students for 2001, the school printed the entire graduating class along the walls near the counselor's office to help inform us of who we needed to sit in between.

Not wanting to face the music but knowing I had to, I walked to the hall of names and before I could even look, my boy Cory comes running towards me out of nowhere and shouts out "WE'RE GRADUATING!". That's right, somehow I made the list!

Graduation came and as an only child, my mom was extremely proud of her son. However, she wasn't aware of how I cheated my way through school. Oblivious to the fact she was proud of a liar, someone that took the credit of other hard-working students.

As fate would have it, out of anyone I could've walked into seconds before I approached the stage I was walking side by side with my algebra teacher of all people. He was one of the chaperones for our graduating class. I shook his hand and told him "thank you". His response was "you know you owe me about thirty dollars right?". He called me out right on the spot face to face, man to adolescent and there was nothing I could do but agree with him. I walked across the stage and fooled everyone who had thought I truly applied myself.

I hadn't applied to any schools nor did I even take my S.A.T.'s. I told my parents I wanted to wait a year before attending college. It wasn't to slack off, I was pretty good at that already. However, I didn't see a point going to school without clearly knowing the purpose. Academics were taken very seriously where my father came from. So my parents agreed to give me half a year off before starting college.

The agreement was that my parents would pay half of my rent as long as I'd stay in school. That only lasted so long. I joined a band called The Kidnap Soundtrack as the guitarist and made music my priority. We practiced every other day and played hundreds of shows, recorded, got signed to a local music label and even toured.

Once I called my dad to borrow some money and he responded with "you only call me when you want something". I don't remember if he hung up on me or if I hung up on him. But that would be the last conversation I had with my father. I blocked him on my phone and labeled him "do not answer". Three full years went by with no contact until my mother had called me and informed me he had a heart attack at work and passed away on site.

You'd think to see my father dead who I purposely neglected for years would have woken me up and set me straight. But after his funeral, it wasn't until father's day 12 years later that I finally went to visit his grave. By this time I was a father myself and after time realized I couldn't ever become the best father I could be because I was still holding onto animosity.

MY WAKE UP MOMENT

It was a little bit before 3:00 AM Monday morning and my phone rang. I've never received a call around this time for anything good and this time wouldn't be an exception. "Terrence I don't know what to do Carl isn't breathing," my mom said. Instantly I woke up and said, "I'm on my way". As I get ready to leave the house with my wife and kids she calls again to relay that he's not responding.

I speed over to my mother's apartment and beat on the door. After about a minute I realized that I had been beating on the wrong apartment door.

For as many years as I've gone to visit my mom you'd think I'd know where she stayed. However, unable to clearly rationalize things I looked over to my right and saw flashing lights from a nearby EMS Truck. As I'm running to it I can't help but wonder why I'm the only person moving with a sense of urgency.

I asked one of the EMT's if my stepdad was ok and the gentleman responded with a simple "he didn't make it". I dart into my mom's apartment to console her and she collapses in my arms.

There's one thing about me, I don't cry much I've even been told many times that I'm emotionless, numb, etc. But my mother is my Achilles heel. All I could remember at that moment was crying and saying sorry a million times as if it was my fault.

Carl aka Fri-dog died in his sleep. Only a few hours after talking and joking around with my mom in the living room. What hurt the most was how unexpected it was, he wasn't catastrophically sick or diagnosed with a life diminishing disease such as my grandmother.

I was so comfortable with him being alive that I never thought of death. I was so comfortable that I didn't know my life was built on the foundation of a rug that can get pulled from beneath me at any given moment.

There I was in the living room face to face with death staring at a man whose wishes, goals and intentions all had an expiration date such as the end of the year aka my birthday December 31st.

THE OUTCOME

When catastrophic things happen in your life you can't help but naturally self-evaluate your current way of living. The death of my stepfather taught me how temporary life really is.

The week proceeded to become an emotional rollercoaster ride. The very next day after Carl's death was my anniversary with the love of my life. Almost a decade went by I realized how much of an idiot I was for not proposing.

Friday the day of Carl's funeral, ironically was same the day my biological dad died 12 years prior and Saturday was my son Hezekiah's birthday.

Everyday life was telling me I had a purpose and the time that I have to live that purpose is shorter than I can ever Imagine. Although the week had been catastrophic, I decided to make my soulmate my life-mate and proposed to my girl, my rock.. Ashley aka "Cheeks" who now also carries the last name of my father.

When I proposed to my wife, I did it with the intention of knowing that I wouldn't have another day to do it.

You can't get anywhere in this life with one foot nailed down to the floor. Too often we don't know the might of our strength until we are truly tested. You are closer than you think to success and the life desired is literally right in front of your face. However, it can't be accessed without hard work and dedication. Take notice, take action and take advantage.

Give yourself credit for the fight and hustle. The soil we stand on is riddled with blood, sweat, and tears from generations of hard work! Each excuse buries who you want to be, where you want to go and diminishes your drive. You must expire your excuses to enhance your expectations. It's time to protest your comfort zone. Let's get started!

If you desire the destination, don't reject the pathway.

Be careful taking one for the team, because you could be the one getting played..

Chapter 1

YOU VS OPTIMISM

Optimism - hopefulness, and confidence about the future or the successful outcome of something.

When did we all become psychics? Everything isn't to be figured out. If you spend all your time finding answers you'll miss out on experiencing life's opportunities and riches.

Are you busy asking questions in which the answers don't drastically change your outcome? We're all guilty of this at some point, which is why it's necessary to notice this early on.

In life, we can unconsciously involve ourselves in conversations and ordeals that don't hold any weight. We somehow instantaneously become detectives, questioning any and everything that enters our minds to evaluate a situation which wasn't our responsibility to resolve in the first place.

Once, while shopping at Target with my wife I overheard an employee asking her coworker if she used the gift card she received at the last meeting. The coworker replied with a simple "not yet".

I thought to myself, why was this question asked and what did anyone gain from it? Perhaps it was just simple conversation and nothing is wrong with that. But when talking to others, it's quite valuable to ask yourself if you're exchanging value or entertainment.

At first thought, providing support and assistance may appear to seem completely innocent and harmless.

However, helping someone out or taking on someone else's problems full throttle can become a very dangerous gesture. It is at this very moment where we invite the chance of negativity to enter into our lives. This behavior is capable of causing domino effects and persuasive cycles, hindering us from success.

What is it inside of us that makes us needy for useless information? What information am I referring to? Any facts, stories, and thoughts that alters your ability to produce benefits in any relatable form to get you where you need to go in life!

Understand that certain problems, people and thoughts will naturally take care of themselves and that's ok. Not everything in the world is your responsibility or right to self willingly take on.

The time you spend analyzing other people's problems only delays you from completing your own tasks.

Calling anyone out on their flaws or transgressions is self-sabotage, stripping you of your grind and focus. Maybe I'm lazy but taking the time to attempt to put everyone in their place seems like a lot of work to do.

Don't make other people's troubles your own. By creating a habit of doing this and being the "go to" person you'll surely advertise yourself as the neverending window of opportunity for someone else.

Learn to cut the bull. We must realize that not everything is relatable to you nor commands your needs to evolve. This isn't a selfish act at all, by doing this over and over you quickly get to the point where you can eliminate the extra baggage in its many hidden shapes and forms.

There's a catastrophically high cost of playing God.

According to the New Testament, Jesus himself originally sent out 70 disciples to go out and spread the word. Do you really wanna take on the world solo? Reach out with your ideas to help bring them to light, you can accomplish more tasks with an open mouth then a closed mind. We're all gifted in certain unique ways. What you must do is find individuals and organizations in which your weaknesses are someone else's strength!

It's ok to admit you're not the most optimal for certain duties. But by obtaining the knowledge to know what's stressful, tedious and time-consuming ahead of time is a very powerful underappreciated characteristic that's simply necessary to succeed.

Have you ever taken time out of your own schedule to provide the most genuine no holds barred advice to a loved one or friend, only for them to completely abandon it and do the total opposite? EPIC FAIL!

Never put yourself in a situation in which you have to shun any well deserved open doors that life has provided for you, in exchange for someone else's gain or temporary happiness.

The same goes with multitasking and micromanaging. Exercise the art of outsourcing. Multitasking is a sure fire way to accomplish low quality work and poor habits. Aim to free up your time to focus on what you love and can do at your absolute best. Perhaps building a team of trusted friends, professionals, and colleagues in different fields will rid you of the mental stress and provide an abundance of freedom.

By continuing to nitpick at yourself with goals of perfection in mind, obstacles will without a doubt use this energy to run circles around you. In fact, perfecting each thought and action you exercise will only create a vicious cycle that'll fester room for distractions, detours and let downs to push through.

If you spend so much time perfecting every step towards your goals you'll never accomplish anything. In fact, you'll take your never-ending projects, goals, desires, hopes and dreams the same exact place more than 90% of the world takes them.. THE GRAVE.

Let's take slavery for example, so many ideas, thoughts, and futuristic innovations were raped, murdered and stolen. What's mind-boggling is the fact that it's almost never discussed. I wouldn't believe it's uncommon to have the mere thought that we as a society are catastrophically behind as a whole, compared to the thought of where we could be currently.

Many slaves and Holocaust victims never had the chance to show who they really were and what they could do. Not only to produce the best versions of themselves but to create, cure and to build legacies. We still don't know exactly how the temples in Egypt were made and how long ago did it happen?

As morbid as it sounds, think about your headstone. Will it say "Jane Doe died with the cure for Cancer", "Never married his/her soulmate", "Battled thoughts of becoming a business owner and lived to mentally beat himself/herself up with unchanging mediocre tasks. While earning money for a cowardly power driven boss 60+ hours a week" (That might be a rather large headstone but you get the point).

This is reality and it isn't by any means over the top, it's actually quite sad how realistic it is. Will your tombstone be epic? Or will you allow all of your innermost ideas to be buried six feet underground just like everyone else?

Embrace the life you live now! The existence of human beings was going on before you were even thought of and will continue once you expire. Life is too short to wonder what could have been. The time is now to leave your mark on the world.

Grab life by the hair and show the world who's in control!

DEVIL'S ADVOCATE

One surefire shortcut to quality mental progression is to play devil's advocate. This naturally forces you to become open-minded. Looking at issues, tasks and feelings from both sides with the worst case scenario in mind will help you in most relationships, jobs and most importantly provide a clearer understanding of who you are becoming as a person.

By using this technique in the employment field you can appear to be compassionate, mature and a step ahead of your coworkers. This could quickly save you from drastically making the wrong decisions and saying the wrong things with your significant other.

It's very important to understand where someone may be coming from in their life but do not waste much time doing so. By quickly picking up on someone's mindset you'll more often than not have all you need to know for proceeding to the next step.

Use this technique before making your next power move so that you'll have to do less backtracking and avoid more problematic scenarios in the future. I'm sure you've heard time is money, however time is not just money. Successful entrepreneurs know that time equals opportunity. You'd be surprised how many people lose out on opportunities and open doors due to an ineffective plan or one-sided mindset.

THOUGHTS & A.C.T.I.O.N.
(Any Change Towards Improving One's Nature)

Thoughts come and go. After time, our mind goes into auto-pilot by doing things in a repeated fashion. It's said that you are what you repeatedly do. But how true is this actually? If you consistently envision thoughts of success you aren't going to get any closer to victory than you were from the jump, that's the dead honest truth that nobody ever tells you.

You can even take it a step further and create the perfect detailed action plan with timelines, deadlines, and goals. Now while this may clearly appear to be a step in the right direction to you, it couldn't be any further from the truth!

Having everything planned out either on paper or digitally should only and I repeat only be used as a monetary reference guide.

Why? Because if whatever you have planned is important and valuable, it will slightly shift or change and you will have to adjust and compensate for the losses. When planning for the future there is absolutely no surefire way to plan for the unexpected twists and turns of life's downfalls, mistakes, slip-ups and failures.

There is no way of psychically being informed to know your progression ahead of time. You will inevitably have to make corrections and alterations. Often you'll hear that having no plan at all is indeed planning to fail. This simple concept and notion is very debatable. You can plan yourself out of organic opportunities. You can unintentionally plan traps and set yourself up for roadblocks. Planning or lack thereof holds little to no weight without action.

It's a hell of a lot easier to dream than it is to succeed. However, by experience, you'll later realize that you can fuse the two together. Success isn't by chance, it comes into your life in only one-way period that's sequential. Success is the result of action. There's cause and effect just as there's action and success. Plan until your heart's content and you'll find yourself still coming up short. The one and only true plan is action period.

Do you think Jimi Hendrix consciously thought about every single note he was going to play ahead of time during a guitar solo? Of course not! You have to step up to the plate take notice, take action and take advantage of your life. What are you waiting for?

Action will always run circles around stagnant concepts detailed or not.

Your thoughts may be to: lose weight, drive a nice car, have financial freedom. These mental insights, dreams or daily tasks remain meaningless without taking the first step. What the guru's keep to themselves is that taking the first step when facing adversity is actually much harder than it is to succeed.

Hold yourself accountable by displaying the act of taking the very first actionable steps towards what you desire in life. Then in a sense, you've already hit all your goals it's at this very moment that you should realize it only becomes a matter of time in which your journey leads you to prosperous fulfillment.

Nothing will be as hard or important as taking the first step.

As I'm sure this all sounds extremely positive and well. I must advise you that action simply does not equate to a smooth journey of discovery and success. In fact, the journey to success isn't often pretty at all. Realistically the road to success is ugly enough to make you want to easily quit and diminish all of your progressive actions.

The two most positive words you will ever need to tell yourself are "Keep going". Get ready because as soon as you take that first step your journey will naturally open up the door to negativity, self-doubt, illusions, and delusions. It's not avoidable at all which is why it's important to remember *what doesn't kill you presently kills the old you previously.*

You are not what or who you once were. As hard as it may appear to seem at first, you're shedding past mistakes and developing a much more mature and knowledgeable mindset to getting to the core that is you. As long as you continue taking actionable steps. No longer will you be defined by your past, it is now the present moment in which your progressive behavior becomes calloused.

Do you realize how powerful this is? The strength and magnitude to naturally display and create such epic quality content by stepping up and taking action compared to only mere thought will get you where you want much faster.

Is your purpose still breathing?

Perfection
Prohibits
Progression

Chapter 2

YOU VS FAILURE

What is failure? Failure is something you create mentally, therefore you have the power to dismiss it. Life is too short to be unhappy. We truthfully never lack the ability to do great things. It's actually incentive, that often picks you back up and motivates you to get the job done when feeling defeated.

Nothing is to gain by giving up, but by doing so you will have everything to lose. Life will never clearly reveal to you that in order to gain success you must fight to succeed just as you'd fight to live.

People will often tell you even if you do not achieve what was originally desired at the end of a challenge, that you'd still come out winning due to the lesson that was learned from the loss.

Be careful, this is a skewed misconception and a very dangerous one at that. This type of acceptance provides an open door to bad habits by numbing the mindset of positive progressive behavior.

A simple pat on the back will not always help you get any closer to slaying your inner dragon.

Ask yourself if you're really happy or just really comfortable. In this life you only have two options: follow someone else's path or create your own. Start focusing on the trends in your life, this is a sure fire way to actually being able to predict the future of where your current lifestyle is taking you.

Get to know yourself:

What's the one thing that would, could or will change your life if you simply tried and succeeded?

Are you willing to never get to where you want because the fear that you made in your mind up is bigger than your dreams?

Get to the source all excuses aside.

Write down the top 5 factors that are hindering you from success (example: time, money, career)

1. _____

2. _____

3. _____

4. _____

5. _____

Congratulations! You now have a blueprint for success! Get comfortable with this list. Put it in your wallet, purse or bathroom mirror.

People spend their entire lives not knowing what sets them back and you've just nailed the issues between you and your goals. A very worthy tool.

Years ago, I worked in the billing department at a psych hospital for the state of Texas and despite my positive efforts, I had a coworker who desired to push my buttons. My mother suggested I write the individual's name or specific issue down on a small sheet of paper, fold it up and put it in my shoe so that I'd constantly step on negativity. Before two months were over I had a new higher paying job.

You've gotta be opened minded to close the door of negativity. (Even if it results in feeling silly, be open to change) One of the aspects that made Michael Jordan a great player was the simple fact that he could maximize the tiniest opportunities. From half a second on the clock to trailing by 6 points.

When was the last time you took monumental action on a pinhole opportunity?

Now that you have pinpointed the obstacles it's time to take actionable steps. It's not as difficult as you think, the hardest part is getting started. It's time to change your way of thinking. Do whatever it takes to get through each challenge that you listed and you'll come to find you're that much closer to obtaining a solid sense of fulfillment.

Afterwards, you'll have the extra confidence and motivation for your future endeavors, knowing that you've self-willingly destroyed prior obstacles. Today is the day you start defining your success. Sometimes the very end of the book tells you all you need to know.

Start backwards, you must realistically connect the future to the present. Many people call this reverse engineering. Don't unify yourself with what you lack, welcome what you aim to evolve. Accept the fact that to get where you want you must never give up, ever.

Get to the point where you can also look at fear as a cop out or a simple excuse to never try. Your attempt at success will always fall short as long as a mentally paralyzed, fear-based mindset exists.

The following are the top three parasites that I'm sure have, will and continue to defeat you if you allow it. These are *self-doubt, negative thinking, and procrastination.*

DOUBTING YOURSELF

Seldom is it discussed but you can be positive and still doubt yourself. Ever take on an opportunity with the best of intentions yet you contain the opposite mindset? It's like going to an interview with the intention of getting hired but feeling that it's an unlikely shot in the dark that you'd actually land it.

Or going up to an attractive person with the hopes of them having mutual interest, but feeling inside that you're gonna get shut down cold. Why do we mentally psych ourselves out?

Why give in to a fallacy that hasn't even happened yet? Remember the Jordan reference from earlier? Sometimes it's the last few minutes of a game that determines the winner and loser. More often than not, **when our back is up against the wall our adrenaline kicks in and we perform above our beliefs and expectations.**

However, many of us never get to this point because we quit before we start. The game's over before you even get to the stadium. Find some guts in yourself and at the very least attempt some kind of action for Christ sake!

NEGATIVE THINKING

(Negate - Nullify; make ineffective)

Do you have the mindset that allows negativity to move in, familiarize itself with your habits and motives only to walk all over you?

Negativity is like an annoying roommate that moves in:

> Gets way too comfortable
> Overstays their welcome
> Never gets the hint
> Takes your self-defeating mindset for weakness

PROCRASTINATION

Anything that doesn't show you the way gets in the way period.

Procrastination is distractions soulmate.

You'll never find the way if you're constantly getting in the way. Screw the natural obstacles you'll have to face for success, it won't matter one bit if you are constantly creating your own pitfalls. Fire the old you and invest in the person you'd like to become.

Hire yourself every day!

FEAR

If you're going to fear anything fear the thought of never trying. What do you honestly have to gain from fear? When has fear benefited you? What have you done in your lifetime to ever become indebted to fear? It's pretty crazy how we can instantaneously and self willingly subject 100% of ourselves to one single emotion. Not just a thought but a nonprogressive, defeating, life decaying mindset.

If you ever wanted to become a millionaire guess what? You've given your millions to fear because it stole your ideas and efforts to make your first dollar. Dreams of quitting your 9 to 5? This is impossible until you first learn to terminate fear's full-time occupation.

We give our passions, careers, finances, hopes and dreams all to fear. *We obey the thought of fear more than we give ourselves the chance to succeed.*

Isn't it ironic how something so small as one simple thought and emotion can have such a monumental impact? Are you guilty of giving your power away to fear every single day?

Fear isn't some gatekeeper that's suppose to strip away any and everything you could have ever hoped to pursue. Fear's prime goal is to make you give up before you even start. We will forever be our own worst enemies.

Stay consistent in your faith because there will come a point in your life where fear will expose the fact that you've been unaware of the true power you have mentally. You have to think of fear as a separate person who appears to always have the upper hand that lies, cheats and steals your innermost desires.

Let's change the way we look at "fear":

Forever Evaluating Anything Reachable

False Evidence Appearing Real

Face Everything And Rise

Foolishly Erasing Any Reasoning

Until you are truthfully striving towards living your passion and sharing your gift with the world, you'll continue to limit yourself to short-term success. To define the future is impossible, the only control you'll ever have is the present.

PROGRAMMING AND CONDITIONING

Are you on cruise control? If so wake up! Don't allow yourself to go through the motions, you've got a life of opportunities to experience new ideas. Be real with yourself and acknowledge your habits and also what pushes you in life. Start reprogramming yourself now.

Are you waiting until your current "circumstances" changes for the better so that you can live a more fulfilling life? Stop telling yourself "one day, when the moment's right, when I have enough money…" Take action by removing such open-ended thoughts from your mind and current vocabulary. Choosing to take this step alone is what will separate you from the goal setters and goal achievers.

Naturally, we create our own current state of affairs and challenges but guess what? They won't change until the proper actionable steps are taken to change them ourselves.

You can wait for a door to open, for the one perfect opportunity that may or may not present itself. But why wait for the door to open, when you can use the hands you have to make an entrance yourself?

What's greater than both money and opportunity? Imagination! The power of imagination is embraced daily as children but as we grow up the ability to continue using this powerful tool is all too often neglected.

As adults, the power to imagine fades and becomes overshadowed with thoughts of school, bills, careers, children and other responsibilities or obligations. We're programmed to live "safe".

The standard we're taught is:

Go to college - this will supposedly lead to a prosperous future.
Obtain a degree - you can only do so much without one.
Land a job - everything can magically fall into place.

Society and the media are both outstanding at camouflaging the continued use of imagination by persuading you that everything that glitters in the form of a 401 K, pension, paid vacation and so on is gold.

Ask yourself, what are you truly contributing?

You could very well be programmed or conditioned without even consciously knowing so. Everyday, people are brainwashed and the thought of simply accepting what society gives you is unfortunately commonly acceptable.

Progressive change is the result of straying from any typical path.

Who's to say your 9 to 5 isn't modern day slavery?

- You're sorted out and picked among others
- You're evaluated and priced
- You're given an employee identification number
- You follow a dress code
- Often assigned to a certain area to work
- Permission must be granted from higher authority to have time off
- Rewarded when expectations are exceeded
- Reprimanded when expectations aren't up to par

Companies hire individuals and they negotiate what their worth is to the company. This act is not often questioned or challenged. How and when did it become acceptable to give into a wage or salary cap when we should look at ourselves as pretty much priceless? Are you worth minimum wage? It's time for some restructuring.

Non-fluctuating repetitional paychecks teaches us how to only value our positions by a wage rather than of its true value. Challenge yourself, without a doubt you would most likely work much harder and effective if you didn't know where the next dollar was coming from. Know what's more disgusting? You're hired to make someone else more money than you'll ever receive.

Corporate America programs you. How can you be pushed to go beyond your current abilities if you're set up to sit comfortably and secure?

Listen up, every morning before you even get out of bed you're awakened with the gift of life. A new pure clean slate everyday you're alive is naturally given to you. How awesome is it knowing you can wake up with a gift?

We often take life for granted. The sad truth is we usually are unaware of what we've come accustomed to especially if it's in abundance. Watch and see how fast you forget who you are once the floor is swept from under you.

DEATH BECOMES YOU

You're more familiar with death than you've taken the time to realize. Are you digging your own grave as we speak?

Let's find out how:

I'm sure you've heard the question before but if you only had 3 days to live only 72 hours, how would you spend it? Have you even taken the question seriously? What do you have to lose by providing an answer with yourself for yourself?

Let's go a step further and dive in even deeper:

If you had only 3 days to live, what specifically in your life would stay the same?

The top three things people intend to change are their finances, careers, and health. These are extremely broad, typical and just plain boring. Nevertheless only you know the answers to these questions that's the beauty in this.

Without blaming anyone else what's really holding you back? Way too many of us are corpses walking around waiting for death, unconsciously inviting it in our households and hearts due to associating your occupation, relationships or lifestyle with the word "hate", boring, defeating, exhausting, etc.

What does that say for yourself? Are you already doing everything you can now to enhance your life? This is a real question you should constantly ask yourself until the answer becomes one with your current lifestyle.

We all have a necessary urge and the reason why your sensors aren't going off is because you've distanced yourself from yourself and your goals.

Chapter 3
YOU VS BAD HABITS

Let's define exactly what habits are and dive into how and why they affect your life.

Habits - the pattern/practice of reoccurring behaviors, thoughts and/or actions.

All good and bad habits are relative. Nowhere in any dictionary will you ever find a relatable reference whatsoever of habits being permanent. Have you ever wondered or even noticed that habits are recurring? They are simply nothing more than "yo-yo challenges", tests and reevaluations that go away just to come right back.

If you consistently throw something at the wall something will eventually stick, and if you throw it with enough force it'll penetrate through the wall.

Decision>Action>Habit>Success

As you can see from the explanation above, habits do indeed have their own role in success. But if you're new to any habit you mustn't look at it as such. You must embrace any forward moving pattern as a "lifestyle change" instead.

UNPRODUCTIVE HABITS

We've discussed how habits and behavioral patterns affect your life, but we can't discount how attractive unproductive habits are as well. With the rise of social media, we are always on edge, wanting to know the latest greatest information at the tip of our fingertips. Having our phones and watches set to alert us to any and everything isn't the way to go.

It is said that it takes about three weeks to form a habit. Three whole weeks! That's twenty-two days, just a week shy of a month. Are you seriously aware of how long this is?

Habits are tricky, which is why it's critical to keep a sense of perspective.

PARALYZED ANALYSIS

Ever been lost and confused in your own thoughts not knowing when to zig or zag? Feeling mentally stuck is ordinarily common, not too much more sucks than putting yourself in your own mental vegetative state.

Paralysis analysis is usually caused by attempting to commit to too many ideas and or tasks.

You'll never be able to get everything done at the same time, you must learn to prioritize. For example, if it's a task on your "to-do" list. Start with the most difficult time-consuming tasks first that way the rest is a breeze. If you're stuck due to an abundance of ideas, this will later come in handy save you time and stress.

AVOIDING A RUT

If you've lived long enough or lived on the edge and came up short there's no doubt you've come to meet hard times.

Let's get into how you can avoid these for the future.

Start
In order to get anywhere, you gotta get the wheels in motion.

Remembering your why
If you don't have a deep-rooted reason to connect your current lifestyle to your goal how can you possibly desire a life worth living?

Don't second guess yourself
Our guts are sometimes smarter than our own minds. If we can't trust ourselves who the hell can we trust?

Positive friends
This can make or break you if you don't have a handle on the goal ahead. Don't allow yourself to let people steal and degrade your goals.

Take breaks
It's never good to get too caught up in something that it holds you back from dominating.

Pride help & lifelines
Pride, it's not something we're at all born with however it is something you acquire through time. Pride is ego's best friend it will destroy clear-cut opportunities due to you not wanting to step outside of yourself.

Some would rather suffer in misery than to reach out for help. What's so bewildering is the fact pride alters your mindset in such a way that you can clearly see opportunity knocking on your door yet still turn it down.

You can be given the green light to success but still, deny it because it's not on your own terms. How idiotically ego driven is this way of thinking? But it happens. Things don't usually seem so stupid until after the act has already happened. This is why it's important to think outside yourself and into a long-term goal.

Be open to help and advice, someone else can present old ideas from angles that were previously unthought of which could spawn new ideas. When pride is at its fullest potential often help is repackaged and labeled as charity. If you want to be successful why not at least be open to the mental gifts of others?

I was going through alot, I was always stuck..
Nobody ever taught me that hard work eliminates bad luck.

Chapter 4
YOU VS CONTRIBUTION

If you yearn to move progressively towards any road that leads to significant fulfillment, it's time to let go of what you're comfortably holding onto. It's only natural to vent, not doing so causes more harm than good. Not allowing yourself to get the steam out will obstacles to find ways to negatively manifest its way into your life.

Ulcers, depression, weight gain, weight loss, fatigue, anxiety loss of desire and medication doesn't sound fun at all does it? Unless you want your inner demons to build and release uncontrollably at any given time, it's suggested you find an outlet or an outcome. (More on this later)

Society has allowed us to self willingly expose more to the world than ever before, from the minor details such as where and what you've eaten to dramatic life-changing ordeals such as childbirth. Some phones even have a built-in camera mode for food! We've welcomed the rise of social media and took it in no holds barred.

Not everything in life is to be shared, and it is your responsibility to play around, explore and find balance. It's not everyone's responsibility to be notified when each and every mediocre self-indulged event has taken place. You'll learn that when you do such things, you expose your vulnerability. Which could be the one thing you need to bridge the gap to success or set ablaze the trail that led you to where you currently are now. Forcing yourself to always move forward.

VENTING TO FRIENDS

"Each friend represents a world possibly not born until they arrive, and it is only by this meeting that a new world is born"
-Anais Nin

Friends are important for the simple fact that they hold the ability to expose characteristics of you that are otherwise hidden. Depending on your friendship/relationship, friends have the ability to yield consistent unfiltered advice.

Friends see you in ways in which you can't see yourself. Wisdom is to be shared not contained, perhaps someone you know has gone through what you're currently dealing with. Sometimes friends have ways of understanding you in which your family never will, with this lies a solid support system. Friends can pick you up when you are down and push you further than you'd ever push yourself.

If you are organically supported by people in your life that mean something to you and hold value, your determination for success can be quite substantial.

However, by opening yourself up and exposing your feelings you must carefully be aware of what you're saying and who you're discussing such things with. Usually, when we feel the need to vent to people it comes out in an unfiltered fashion, this could potentially become very detrimental in later times.

VENTING TO NEGATIVE PEOPLE

Let's just be honest and keep it 100%. Not everyone has your best intentions and the ones who have the potential to do the most harm are typically the ones that are closest to you.

Pay attention to who and when you decide to display your reactions. **Your negative energy could be the fuel that lights the fire of a detrimental future.** The individual listening could be in a bad state of mind already and their thoughts could influence yours in a way that's completely out of your character. You'll find that negative people feed on negativity as if its a buffet.

Negative mindsets are constantly recruiting members. Keep a mental list of not only negative driven people but what sets them off as well. They may be unaware of their tone and demeanor but why give them the power to influence your decisions or future? Sounds like common sense right? You'd be surprised how issues suddenly become foggy and grey. Quite often the closer someone is to you the more weight their opinions, thoughts, and views hold.

GROWING SEEDS, BECOMING BELITTLED AND BACKDOORED

Never allow people to throw seeds at you. There will without a doubt come a time when people will see your positive progression, the more success you endure the more life with test you to make you grow stronger.

Success will be difficult to see at the beginning. This is the perfect time for haters to ensue in the form of obstacles to hinder the process of you getting to where they will never go. Let's call them "seeds".

You can fall into traps that allow you to water and nurture all dilemmas which will eventually grow into deep seeded roots of a failure mindset. Eliminate the negative people in your life, it's only wasted energy that you could use towards your goals.

Life's short, never let negative people who aren't open-minded impregnate you with their dead-end mindsets.

WHAT'S YOUR OUTLET?

What's your outlet? Do you have a go-to source whether it's private or public where you can truly 100% be yourself, unjudged? What makes you feel "at home" with yourself? Perhaps your "happy place" beings and ends simply with a pen and pad.

Everyone needs some sort of goto source in which one can uniquely penetrate their inner talents.

"To be yourself in a world that is constantly trying to make you something else is the greatest accomplishment"
-Ralph Waldo Emerson

It's interesting how as young adolescents we're often told we can be anything we want when we grow up. But no one tells you how mind-boggling and catastrophically important it is to start figuring out who you are right now!

As adults too often that notion has long faded away. Or even worse.. we grow up becoming hypocrites, stressing to our youth the importance of pursuing a talent or passion while we're currently working jobs where we're just another number. Disliking the decisions we've made ourselves.

How well do you know yourself? Do you spend so much time consumed in negativity and drama that you've become a stranger to yourself? Understand how you handle situations because it's a necessity in a forever changing world.

This is your life, are you who you want to be?

Let's do a self evaluation ask yourself these questions:

Do you feel like you've lived this day a hundred times before?

At what time in your recent past have you felt most passionate and alive?

If we learn from our mistakes, why are you always so afraid to make them?

What do you love? Have any of your recent actions openly expressed this love?

What would you do differently if you knew nobody would judge you?

When is it time to stop calculating risk and rewards, and just go ahead and do what you know is right?

What do I have to offer my family, friends and most importantly myself?

Do you typically find yourself spending more time doing what you don't enjoy and talking about issues you dislike rather than what makes you happy?

It's time to start asking yourself how you got into these situations.

Be honest with yourself and figure out if you may have possibly allowed these things to manifest into your lifestyle. *Your stolen aspirations may have been self-induced.*

**Check yourself
don't reject yourself.**

When you have a strong "why"..
it'll naturally roll out the red carpet for your "how".

Chapter 5
YOU VS SETBACKS

Are you a quitter? I'll never forget, I was a sophomore in high school and my grandmother was diagnosed with breast cancer. Believe it or not, I didn't know much about cancer at the time or exactly what it was.

My grandmother went through the regular chemotherapy process. She lost her hair, her skin gradually got darker and she became physically weak. There was even a time she yelled my name from downstairs due to a fall in the bathroom. But she continued to battle this disease.

After a year of fighting, my grandmother stood up in church and announced her breast cancer was in remission. However a few months later it came back.

Now I'm not sure if the cancer came back more aggressively, but it didn't matter much because it had done so much prior damage. What I'm saying is you are one idea, one move, one statement from solidifying your demise or your destiny.

My grandmother died fighting, she would have left this world a lot sooner had she given up. You see my grandmother had no option but to fight, her life literally depended on it.

Stop acting like you have options. My goal for this book is to expose ideas in ways that force you to take action.

Perhaps you've done so much hard work that you only need that one final push to finish, but instead you quit. **If you're going to give up you've got no business starting in the first place.**

Don't doubt yourself to the point where you give failure and rejection the power to make decisions for you.

You don't know what your success number is. If you've been rejected 100 times maybe it's the 101 attempt that will lead to success.

You must understand the rejections you receive now will lead you to the rewards you'll have later.

> "We're all self-conscious I'm just the first to admit it"
> — Kanye West

If you choose to see it as an option, the option to quit will always be there. So will the opportunity to postpone things. You may always have the option to go left, right, up or down. But with information, opportunities and outcomes its vital that you pay the most attention to what goes in and out.

The truth is nothing ever gets easier, the only thing that changes are your options. You literally have the power to create or eliminate them. Mostly everyone who's experienced success through the test of time continues to do so due to their mindset, their option is to have no option.

In Bruce Lee's famous movie *Enter The Dragon,* there's a very popular scene where he's with a student who delivers a very flawed sidekick.

Bruce Lee tells the student:
"A good fight should be like a small play, but played seriously. A good martial artist does not become tense, but ready. Not thinking, yet not dreaming. Ready for whatever may come. When the opponent expands, I contract. When he contracts, I expand. And when there is an opportunity, I do not hit. It hits all by itself."

Can you imagine practicing something to the point in which it becomes its own entity and takes a life of its own?

Think of where you're at right now...
Think of what you're wearing...
Think of what you're reading...
Think of what you're driving...

Any and everything you have was once based on a thought and a blueprint or model. Bring your ideas to life.

Think > Execute > Experience

You should demolish any options and thoughts that don't require hard work, as they may very well lead to a mirage of unhappiness.

Options can be dangerous just ask Wall Street. No risk no reward is true. But what's the use if the risk is no longer substantial?

Now I'm going to really need you to stay with me here.

Everyone including you reading this book right now already have the body you've been dreaming of. The reason why it doesn't look ideal to you right now is that you've accepted the wrong self-image. You gotta see the six-pack mentally before you can obtain the six-pack physically. What made Steve Jobs and Apple important was that to succeed they knew they had to see what others couldn't. Let's not forget *we thrive on artificial visualization.*

Before you got to where you are currently, did it start with a vision? Perhaps you're like me, maybe you didn't see it yourself, it was all around you but remained unnoticed. We can all be naive, but **the tools you need for success are often hidden in plain sight.**

You are a fighter! Too often we don't pat ourselves on the back. When's the last time you could just bask in the glory of an accomplishment? Take a step back and REALLY look at the obstacles life has presented you. Give yourself credit for the fight and hustle. The soil we stand on is riddled with blood, sweat and tears from generations of hard work!

Your B.S. (Belligerently Stupid) Dilemma

The only thing that will confirm rejection is the lack of consistent action.

You are living your opportunity. You are your outcome. If you want to become the next bodybuilding pro, actor, football player, if you wanna land that new job, start a relationship and live what you only have dreamed. Listen up..

I had an epiphany and felt the need to elaborate even further so that it can hit home. Open your eyes and be willing to step back, often you'll realize you are in your own way.

No matter what it is in life that you want to conquer it's literally yours, you just have to want it enough and pay attention to the signs life provides for you. Often the signs are literally right IN FRONT OF YOUR FACE. I believe life has a way of providing you with what you desire, it's just a matter of honing in and focusing on the signs for your taking.

You already own that million dollar contract, endorsements, the house of your dreams is already built and ain't NOBODY living in it yet, that person you've been crushing over is already yours. But are you gonna be all in? I know it all sounds easy, doesn't it? Well, it should! Why?

I'll let you in on something.. I'm sure you've heard. "If it was easy everyone would do it".

That's the biggest load of crap I've ever heard! Technology has advanced us in such a way where everything is EASY.

* It's easy to be lazy
* Easy to be comfortable being comfortable
* Easy to delay tasks with Netflix & social media

* Easy to put things off & go to sleep
* Easy to blame others for not accomplishing goals
* Easy to simply give up
* Easy to keep things easy

It is EASY and everybody IS already doing it! (It being "nothing")
You could have a personal trainer for FREE and literally give up
before you've made an honest attempt.

People reject and often treat "free" like it's an embarrassment.

"Easy" is a mindset.
Let's have a quick rapid fire Q&A:

Wanna get rich? = Live like you're broke
Wanna lose weight? = Eat healthy and exercise
Wanna be more attractive? = Find out what others desire
Are you Hungry? = E.A.T.! (Endure Attain Transpire)
Wanna raise? = Perform higher than your expectations or ask.

Think "Netflix", how much does it cost to go to the movies or
buy a dvd? Netflix is cheaper than a date at the movies and pays for
itself pretty much instantly. Netflix perceives to provide more value
than the cost so people will always pay a fixed price every month, for
years due to the value.

Do you over-deliver in any area of your life?
You see, logically on paper it seems pretty black and white.
However, just like our alphabets, we try to go from A to Z and self
willingly omit everything in between. Which is what bridges the gap.

I once had a supervisor who wouldn't let us ask questions unless
we had proof we had previously exhausted all of our options. Truth is
things are getting easier yet we still hesitate and remain stagnant.

If you have that gut feeling that your current relationship, career
or whatever situation you may be in is fleeting... chances are it is. You

don't need to get approval from anyone but yourself. All anyone else will do is tell you what you already know.

It's funny how often things don't resonate until someone says out loud what we've already told ourselves inside.

Life will align you with your purpose, but the way in which life presents it won't be sexy at first or a neon flashing sign but in due time you'll too have that "duh" moment. I'm not going to bore you with any numbers but it's often said we do not use 100% of our brain. I'd have to agree but it's not as if we don't have the ability to do so. The problem is, we as humans are often enablers. We fail at failing.

SEEING YOUR FUTURE

It's not a matter of being psychic some even say it's God that allows you to see things and while I'm not exactly sure that's true, I do know you have to go all in and go hard.

How often do you get that feeling where you tell yourself:

"something about this just ain't right"
"Something's telling me..."

This series of synapsis isn't only your mind. It's the result of the numerous signs life has placed around you that continue to be ignored.

The opportunities to succeed are literally all around you they come to you in many shapes, forms and fashions. 99% of the time you will NEVER self-willingly take the chance as long as you dismiss them. You'll pass up the key ingredient to the recipe, you'll shun that job opportunity and you'll blindly ignore consistent details.

We are programmed to see red flags as signs of danger.. not all of the signs life presents you with are negative, you MUST get to a point where you see these flags for what they really are! You will always be your own worst enemy. You MUST believe the only person that can get in your way is you! Being adventurous will take you far in life.

There isn't a person on this planet that isn't consumed with unanswered questions. But if you took the time to write down 10-20 problems or irritants I'm 100% sure you'd have some of the issues resolved in your mind before you even wrote the problem down on paper.

I hope you can see where I'm going with this. My whole point is, your issue isn't an issue at all. This is how you make a dollar outta 15 cents. You allow the truth to hurt.

Once you can get a grip and bring awareness to your awareness the world is literally yours.

Right & wrong will always make themselves present.

If you only focus on what you can get,
you'll lose out on what you can give.

Chapter 6
YOU VS SELF

To dreamers, results often outlast integrity. But people who don't sleep know their purpose.

I personally do not believe it's stressed enough but when is the last time you've done a self-examination? It's necessary in a forever changing world.

* How well do you know yourself?
* When's the last time you've gotten to know yourself?
* Have you truly embraced yourself?

Are you consumed with work and the drama it may come with? If you're dreading the work day based on certain individuals what does that say about you? You may have become so consumed in their lives, in their personality that you don't even know who you are anymore. You may know more about someone else than yourself. Who are you?

This was the case for me in school, my motto was "it's better to cheat than to repeat". I never placed myself in a position to be good at anything because I'd quit anytime I met resistance. As a result, I forfeited my identity.

Becoming aware of it and constantly asking yourself questions is a good step in the right direction.

Ever find yourself stuck in a rut? A routine? If this is the case, you'll soon find that we only receive back what we put out into life.

Ever find yourself asking these questions?

-Do I have any energy after work to actually do something for myself?
-Should I cook when I get home or just grab some fast food?

As if traffic to and from work wasn't enough, you find yourself slowly becoming a ticking time bomb by the time you get home and walk through the door.

Like a spring trap, just waiting for someone to say or do the wrong thing so that you can unleash the wrath of utter frustration that's been building up because you had a bad day, a resolution that didn't fall in your favor.

If you've often found yourself in such previous situations...Guess what??? SOMETHING'S WRONG!!!! It's actually at this moment where you need to start being honest with yourself and questioning everything.

Get to the source!!! Often you'll find that you self-willingly put yourself in situations that you now REGRET or are unhappy with. Stress causes many things: weight gain, weight loss, high blood pressure, fatigue, loss in sexual desire (you can't be afraid to address this), alcoholism, panic attacks, depression, heart attacks, and can ruin relationships and families.

Eliminate the precursor and you could eliminate having to go to the doctor and getting OVERCHARGED for ailments you could have avoided in the first place.

We're very quick to judge others before we judge ourselves.

How "on point" have YOU been lately?

Betrayed beliefs

=

buried blessings

If you go to sleep on your goals, your habits will tuck you in.

Chapter 7
YOU VS CONSCIOUSNESS

Pay close attention to your consciousness, because what you may not hear in your head will eventually become physically present.

Sometimes when you're focused on a goal you get insanely inspired, however with that inspiration comes the ability to lose yourself.

You can write things down, set reminders on your phone basically attempt to prepare yourself as much as you want but it won't prepare you for the directions, twists, and turns of life.

Daily planners can get lost and phones can die, life has made these things so simple that you can quantify what you need simply by voice commands.

Why are we so busy? Are we REALLY this busy? How did we as humans become so occupied that we need assistants to grab us coffee, lunch, shop for us, etc.

Are you living a life with uncontrollable deadlines? Deadlines on tasks that aren't aligned with your passions and desires? Is it a life or death situation to update your Facebook, Instagram or Twitter? Is everything and everyone in your life strictly on a need to know basis?

If you find it difficult to get things done it's because the distractions in your life aren't just simple distractions. You're actually allowing yourself to be controlled in a micro-sense! Chances are you didn't see this coming. You are now sitting down on things you can't stand. But more importantly, now that you know.. WHAT ARE YOU GOING TO DO ABOUT IT???

Years ago daily planners didn't exist. If mom told you to grab something from the grocery store you either wrote things down on paper and kept a Kung Fu grip on the list, or you simply remembered with your mind.

We have become a barcode driven, voice-activated, GPS navigated, downloadable, cloud-based society! If you were to lose your cell phone and you were in need of help how many phone numbers would you remember? If you went to jail for whatever reason and you were given that one free call what would you do?

How often are we in situations in which we say "I know I'm forgetting something"? There's just that uncomfortable feeling of neglect. We can remember to remember things, however, we can't recall what exactly to remember. Which brings me to my point.

Whenever that synapse first arrives, ACT ON IT! This is called the speed of implementation. These thoughts are often like coupons or sales, they're only available for a limited amount of time and if you don't take advantage soon you'll lose it.

Why leave an idea in your mind only to later become forgotten? You may be in the same boat as myself, where ideas arise just as often as they fleet away.

Follow your original mindset, trust your instincts period!

The further we travel into technology the more we lose ourselves. So break free of what's enabling you to be distracted. The race isn't won with just the effort alone, it takes discipline as well.

Don't allow yourself to take the easy way out. If weeding out distractions presents a challenge, take it on and be prepared to be unprepared.

Aim to open your eyes and mind, break the habit of putting things aside and realize chances are you're less likely to forget something that greatly affects your life in a positive manner.

Always remember your lifestyle should greatly resolve around your purpose.

DIRECT DEPOSIT HAPPY

When you know money is coming in, you have a huge sense of happiness. Nobody can ever break that feeling you have inside. You can literally go to bed feeling broke and wake up feeling rich regardless of the amount. Why? Because it's simply more than what you had previously.

A small victory after a big war is just as monumental as it is crucial. Regardless of the amount, just knowing that you have guaranteed money puts you in a mental state of euphoria.

I need you to direct that same feeling and same emotion towards the goals you have yet to accomplish.

I need you to be happy about the lessons you've learned from coming up short.

I need you to be direct deposit happy when your boss tries to break you down.

I need you to be direct deposit happy when the day doesn't seem like it can get any worse but you're determined to change that around and dominate.

I need you to be direct deposit happy in your relationships.

I need you to be just as happy in the attempt to conquer your fear.

I need you to be direct deposit happy when you meet resistance and things don't go your way.

Why? Because when you're direct deposit happy you already know what the end goal is. You know what it takes to get what you want, being direct deposit happy is the result and confidence of knowing that your efforts will be handsomely rewarded.

Being direct deposit happy allows you to work in a resilient atmosphere and allows your tunnel vision to take you to the next level.

Direct deposit happy is all about your internal drive.

But you can't be direct deposit happy with overdraft tendencies.

You gotta be careful how much you withdrawal in life, why? Because it's crucial that you don't dwell on the excitement of your goals.

When you share and teach what's helped you in life you develop an interest and expertise in that particular topic. This interest provides extra value.

So I need you to be direct deposit happy with everything that you do I need you to know your purpose is bigger than you.

Your journey is a direct deposit to your destination.

BACKUP PLANS

I was so worried about holding myself back in school that I held myself back in life.

How can you ever give 100% in anything with even something as little as a 1% thought of failure? The danger with a backup plan is you risk setting yourself up for an unfulfilling lifestyle. Quite often we're told by our parents especially if you want to do something outside of working at a desk... "Make sure you have something to fall back on".

As if you already failed or might fail. Where's the motivation???

Let's just admit it, a backup plan is designed by the thought of the original plan not working. It's a "safety net" or "just in case" if you will. A backup plan is like a cheat meal, it's designed by someone who refuses to go all in.

Your backup plan sucks! Here's why:

The more backup plans you have the less likely you are to succeed at your original goal. Why would you want anything less than linear at your disposal?

Backup plans are uniform and sequential. If you settle for average you'll do average things. You'll learn to teach average skills and pass them down to your average children. You'll show your boss an average work ethic, resulting in an average evaluation and your paycheck will reflect it.

Some things in life can't be replaced and one thing that should never be replaced is what you truly unconditionally love and desire.

Chances are your backup plan was nothing more than a second place avenue. Nobody purposely wants the silver medal, how would you feel if your significant other was replaced with a "runner-up"?

Imagine going to a concert to see your favorite band only to realize you were misinformed and that you actually came to see a "cover band" play your favorite band's top hits!

What do you believe? When it comes down to it, a backup plan is nothing but the result of false hope.

If you've been lucky enough to find your calling you know without a doubt it's irreplaceable, let that be symbolic of your mission and efforts.

SEIZE THE MOMENT

Many of us know what we want but don't know who we are.

We've heard it all before, "carpe diem" or "Seize the day". Who actually lives by this philosophy though? People who have succeeded and continue to do so that's who. One of the reasons why it sounds so cheesy is due to the increasing lack of action and accountability you might have.

PAY ATTENTION

Sounds like an insanely simple statement. We gotta catch ourselves because we often overlook the obvious. But there's more to it, whenever you pay "attention" to anything it's necessary that you don't come up short.

Once the wife and I argued the first 5 minutes into an hour and a half route to a waterpark.

The way I look at it, we had **two options:**

Option 1: Spend the trip dwelling on justifying a misunderstanding.

Option 2: Move past this lesson and embrace the ability to enjoy some quality family time.

Your time and attention are two of the most valuable commodities you have and you don't want to waste it on obstacles that provide little to no value in return.

Don't handicap yourself by staying stuck on the problem. Say goodbye to your comfort zone. As mentioned before we were on our way to a water park, once we arrived at the lazy river it was time to get in, but as we all know, that initial encounter with the water temperature is quite an adjustment.

Not knowing how cold the water was I stepped in knee deep, it sent a shock through my entire nervous system, telling my brain to resist and "ease" my body into the cold river.

I pushed passed my comfort zone and literally submerged myself in it from head to toe. It sucked initially but a few seconds later my body adapted to the temperature. Which brings me to my point.

Don't fear challenges, embrace them because behind every challenge is a progressive opportunity to succeed.

Whether you're at a meeting or in a classroom, when someone speaks what's one of the first things you're likely to do? Are you quick to jot things down? If so, you omit the ability of any natural connection to the person speaking and their words. Instead, be brave and actually listen.

You're more likely to remember the things that stand out and resonate with you.

We all have that one friend or family member who MUST take pictures of EVERYTHING. Maybe you're that person. Nothing annoys me more than someone telling me I can't eat my food until they take a picture of it.

So many of us get lost in the attempt to capture current moments that we ironically miss the BIG picture and lack the use of all the 5 senses. There's no app required to live life.

Why create something you can't connect to?

Your maximum effort might be someone's minimum requirement.

Chapter 8
YOU VS DEADWEIGHT

Does your desire outweigh your efforts? The quickest way to dropping the dead weight long term is to define what's urgent and what's nonessential. Determine if you're majoring in insignificant tasks that do not align with your end goals or if you're actually minoring in the significant factors that will drive you to your destination.

Maybe you have a baby-sized grind and an adult size dream.

It's natural to dream big. Who doesn't want to be two steps ahead in every aspect of their lives and have an extra digit in their bank account? No matter how solid your commitment is, carrying around dead weight will hinder your dreams.

Distractions are like fast food, you receive instant gratification but also obtain long-term weighted problems.

When's the last time you turned your phone OFF not restart but actually off? Ever use "do not disturb" or airplane mode?

When do you turn the tv off? When it's time to get ready for work or go to bed? What are you majorly spending your time doing? What are you giving your big efforts to? Ever binge watch tv shows? (Even if it's only every now and then) Get a grip on these questions and you might just find your own Achilles heel.

The biggest secret that attracts us to distractions is instant gratification. We look forward to the "likes" and attention we gain from Facebook, Instagram, Twitter, etc. Often this is what we exchange our precious time for.

The problem isn't that you can't accomplish what you want, the issue is that often the small gratification from social media doesn't yield long-lasting results. It's the difference between a one night stand and a long satisfying marriage.

PROCRASTINATION ISN'T A DISEASE!

Never allow comfort to come into your life and stray you from the path by pushing you further away from your goals. At this point, it's time to reevaluate and reassess your directional path.

Grab a sheet of paper and write down what you're an expert in

(Hint: Anything you can typically teach, give a course on or write a book on. This includes social media and tv shows)

1. **Cross out EVERYTHING you think gets in the way of what you truly desire**

2. **Circle the ONE category you're an expert in that can accelerate you to your goals.**

3. **Whatever your ONE thing is, write it down, put it in your wallet, purse, bathroom, car, office, etc.**

From this point on if you pay close attention, you'll notice your mind will naturally search for any and every distraction under the sun, life will test your consistency and it's up to you to exhaust yourself with the dead weight or lighten your load and accelerate your life to obtain greatness. We live in a world where "Nobody wants to climb" anymore we'd much rather segway and hovercraft our way to success.

This comes at a price...

BRIDGING THE GAP

Alright, so you're at the point where you believe you know where you're going in life. I'll commend you on this. That in itself is a gigantic step in the right direction. A "purpose" in general is a vital objective that many people honestly take years to obtain and find themselves becoming lost in the search. Now while this would all seem fine and dandy, on the contrary, it is actually far from I'll explain...

Take a moment to think about it, we have to work to become what we "want to be" by typically investing thousands of dollars, and hundreds of hours in education. Sure, we're not born knowing what our life's evolutions will amount to. But perhaps if we took the time to listen to our wants, needs and effortless talents we'll discover the answer.

Uncertainty will manifest itself into your daily habits if you lack clarity you'll unconsciously give away your precious time in exchange for distraction.

I myself have a small personal library. However, I don't allow an abundance of information to become an obstacle. Never allow yourself to get so caught up and attached that you miss the opportunity to take action whether it's a crush you currently have, job, life journey or question that needs to be addressed.

In the time that you're reading, studying, going to seminars, watching videos on youtube, etc. You could be doing actual work.

"I fear not the man who has practiced 10,000 kicks once, but I fear the man who has practiced one kick 10,000 times"
— Bruce Lee

What's something you want so bad you'd be willing to risk anything for it? Let's just put money into the scenario now stay with me..

If you could get paid a dollar for every push up you could do would you make time to do the push-ups? Would you drop everything right now and do them? What would your ideal number be? Would you go balls to the wall, knocking out as many as you could do until your body collapsed?

Most of us would push ourselves past our limits. If you want something bad enough you'll make time for it. Not having time is no longer an excuse.

Once you finally find your calling and your life's purpose the destination soon starts. It's important to find the tools that will get you from point A to point B.

Typically one doesn't know exactly how things will pan out. Most don't know where to start so I say work backward you'll find it much easier and motivating than starting from scratch.

Instead of writing down steps to get to your goal write down the steps as if you've already obtained it until where you are currently.

Here's an example:

9. Gain revenue
8. Sale
7. Marketing
6. Obtain a website to drive the product or service to the forefront
5. Outsource what can't be done or what occupies the most time
4. Create product or service
3. Obtain a team of like-minded goal driven individuals
2. Vision a lifestyle, company or product
1. Find a problem to solve

Of course, this is a very mild non-detailed example but you get the point. Try Fail Win Period.

Face it
and
finish it.

Chapter 9
YOU VS HUSTLE

Here's why you should hustle. Winners win and losers lose. If you've got time to catch up on your favorite tv shows, movies, social engagements and you're complaining then you are simply the cause of your own demise let's be honest.

Do you think the lack of a 4-year degree and graduate school is the reason why you aren't earning what you feel you deserve?

Well, that's simply not true! Is a financial burden getting in the way of your dreams? If so, I'll tell you the truth and you better listen up because the truth doesn't always make itself easily available to you. The only reason why you don't have what you desire is because you've given it away!

Let me explain, you can never make up for lost time. So the time you have now is catastrophically crucial! If you're a living breathing human I'm sure you've faced regret, what's worse is regretting a decision after seeing the yielded results (what you could have had).

How many times have you told yourself the following:
I should have...
I could have...
I would have...
If only…

What's stopping you from trusting yourself? Fear? It blows my mind how people fear things they've never tried. I don't get it, how can you be afraid and allow yourself to mentally fail at something you've never even attempted??? As if you've already gone out and attempted the endeavor.

Stop doing things that don't resonate with your purpose.

At the very least go out and physically fail, I recommend it. When's the last time you failed at something without gaining new knowledge you didn't have prior? If you fail you'll have a lot more to say for yourself and the effort at the least displays integrity. Simply not trying exposes your inner coward! Whether you consider the odds are against you or not is meaningless if you aren't producing any odds at all.

We all would like to make money in our sleep that's typically 8 hours your bank account is pretty much frozen and stale. **Many things that you're attracted to are actually in some sense indebted to you.** Why do you think artists and celebs usually thank their fans?

I'll explain, the tv shows you watch, books you read, music you listen to everything that you usually consume "provides" goods and services due to the "demand" which is you! By being a consumer, others succeed based on the demand in which you provide.

However, don't expect to get a check from all the hours of The Kardashians, The Walking Dead or Breaking Bad you might've watched. In fact, they're spending the money you're providing them right in front of your own face!

From the views and free word of mouth marketing and promotion that you provide them. What's the return on investment? Another season for you to watch? I'm not saying you shouldn't watch tv and indulge in entertainment every now and then but if you're not where you want to be you should know exactly why.

HERE'S HOW TO HUSTLE:

This means waking up earlier than the ones currently on top of the ladder. For example, the average person reads only one book a year but more importantly did you pay attention to what I just said? The "average person".

You didn't come across this book by accident, something drew you to it you aren't average so stop associating yourself with that word and anyone that displays this type of behavior.

You can't kill a hustler Why? It's very difficult to kill something that's constantly moving.

"Hustling is like playing a video game with a cheat code that allows you to be invincible, kicking butt and taking names plowing through obstacles to get to your destination"

1. Throw away practicality as it has the chance of limiting the vision of what you desire because your dreams and drive should NEVER have a capitation.

2. Define what you want

3. Assume and vision that you'll obtain whatever it is, forget plan b don't set yourself up for a handicap. Go out and do it (bring a notepad and a pen wherever you go, if you fail you can jot down notes and reverse engineer if you succeed you can jot down notes and create steps moving forward)

4. Consistently repeat the process until what you desire is literally staring you in the face!

Sleep doesn't care about your goals and most likely your boss doesn't as well let's just be honest.

ADVANTAGES TO HUSTLING:

Consistency - You can't lose if you never give up point blank period! By being consistent you build a hard exterior, which further prepares you for future obstacles.

Results & rewards - Hustler's are rewarded as the result of taking action.

Confidence - Once you make the first sale, get the first degree, land that job you'll have the mental ammo you need to succeed.

Drive - The biggest and most effective tool to hustling is your grind and your direction there's only one direction.. FORWARD hustlers know why they grind and what they hustle for.

Knowledge - This is your monumental advantage, people can educate themselves with books and videos, they can even surround themselves with like-minded individuals but nothing at all holds as much as weight as experienced knowledge. There's just simply some skills you can't learn and obtain from a book.

Networks - If you hustle long enough you'll meet individuals and organizations that may provide additional opportunities and perhaps even take you under their wing, you risk the chance of being at the right place at the right time.

Outsourcing - Once you get a handle on things you'll learn to outsource and use other resources to do certain tasks for you saving you time, stress and providing you the freedom to move onto the next goal. If the business can't run without you physically doing the work it simply means you don't have a "business" you have a "job". When's the last time you saw the founder or CEO at your job?

Never let your mouth... overdraft your actions.

When comfort's your habit, success can only be sporadic.

Chapter 10
YOU VS SECURITY

How secure are you with the things going on in your life right now? Unsatisfied?

You've been taught to believe you were a virgin however..
Every idea and action impregnates the next.

You've been impregnating thoughts, ideas and actions long before you knew you were able to. Most people that are successful didn't obtain it simply out of nowhere. Success is sequential.

The life you live is nothing but the result of past actions

By consistently hitting the gym you'll obtain a healthy body. I didn't know what confidence was until I start taking martial arts, striving for my black belt provided me with a platform to obtain the confidence I didn't have previously.

By consistently reading how to better yourself you'll obtain greatness and people may even look at you as an expert simply because you stand out. You'll have an advantage and become a source people will go to due to your vast wealth of knowledge.

If you suck at basketball yet commit to 1000 jump shots every day 7 days a week for just two weeks do you know how much of an advantage you'd have? Do you see on consistency works? Take notice.

Stop suffering

Have you settled and are you insanely comfortable with your current lifestyle even though it sucks! You aren't rich because you lack the ability to generate substantial income, what you lack is the will and knowledge. Do your excuses outweigh your actions.

You're taught to adapt and accept. Do you remember those little Venn diagrams we used as kids? When's the last time you even heard of a Venn diagram? Remember cause & effect, compare & contrast, main idea vs details?

As kids we're taught to use our creative thinking. You had the ability to create stories, characters, use your imagination and explore. Back in my day we used macaroni to create things. Even with our childhood toys, we did so much with so little (I'm an 80's baby).

Imagination would literally go on for hours with just one toy. Howeverrrrr as we grow older the very notion of "imagination" or "creativity" slowly fades away to the point where it's nonexistent in middle school and high school.

Imagination gets replaced with systematic structures.

If not detected early on, this becomes the way things are done in your life. **You become so mentally numb and calloused from going by the book that you start to develop a sense of scarcity for anything off kilter, unstructured and unplanned.** Anything that strays from the normal path typically makes you feel uncomfortable and unconfident. You naturally settle, because you've been conditioned to do just that.

Life is only as difficult as we make and allow it to be. It's pretty nutty how people follow the dumbest trends that don't matter yet are blind to the ones that are life changing and they're RIGHT IN FRONT OF OUR FACE.

Do you know how both celebrities and entrepreneurs obtain power, money, fame and become the 1%? They strayed from the path! They broke the cycle, dared to be different. That's it that's the trend that's "the secret".

The reason why you'll spend $$$ discovering the secret to success is because the majority of us have the wrong perception of it to begin with. You don't want success, you only want what successful people have accomplished.

Yet if you actually obtained millions of dollars or a fancy house chances are you'd lose it. Because you'd lack the journey or experience to maintain and that alone is PRICELESS.

We usually NEVER weigh the rejection, heartache, bankruptcy, addiction, divorce, ect. as high as we do the success. You can't sell rejection it's not sexy.

Success is nothing but a ball..
Sometimes it goes down the gutter

Gets fumbled
Hit with a bat
Gets rejected or intercepted
But the ball always goes in the direction of the goal.

The only secret is HARD WORK but it LITERALLY goes out of 99% of everyone's ears it sounds too easy, too black and white and just plain boring. You can't sell hard work it's not sexy either.

Degrees aren't guarantees

When you're not doing what you're put on this earth to be doing you're likely being paid to serve someone else's purpose. All forms of education are great to be quite honest however... Many obtain degrees with the mindset that completion will lead to bettering themselves, opening doors, having options and more money.

However, clarity comes from action not only your thoughts and ideas. Degrees do not guarantee you a job, they are however tied to debt. It can be taxing to find an occupation where you aren't interrupted, distracted and redirected. But nevertheless, our body structures were not designed to sit down 8 hours a day.

I've had jobs where business development managers and department directors with doctorates we're so book smart that they couldn't do something as simple as faxing a document. Happens ALL the time.

Nobody writes about you in a history book unless you do just that, make history.

If your mother came to you hungry would you let her starve or would you feed her? You'd quite naturally take action and provide her with the food you feel she desperately needs. Why don't you take the same kind of natural action into what you really want to do with your life?

Leave the bs at the door and decide to grow up.
Starting today you will leave behind those damn shoulda woulda coulda's. Starting today you will realize fear is nothing but what you imagine in your mind.

Action is what separates the spectators and the go-getters
It's time to stop getting in your own way and make a decision
Are you doing anything currently to better your life? Most of us just stop at this question.. What's the damn harm in thinking things through?

The lack of attempts to finding a solution or resolution to your thoughts is reflective of how you actually implement other situations in your life as well.

If you maintain incomplete thoughts, you'll do incomplete work.

Stop selling yourself short and embrace the present moment. Most of us including myself at one point worked jobs that paid just enough to keep you from quitting and as a result you worked just enough to keep from being fired.

If this sounds similar to you and your situation understand that you're just cheating yourself.

Stop using the word "predict" and replace it with "expect" We aren't living predictions we're simply LIVING PRESENTLY. You can go to school and educate yourself all you want, get the degree and predict you'll make X amount of money. Maybe you will maybe you won't but I GUARANTEE there will be something that finds its way into your life that you could have never predicted.

Don't get lost in "setting up" for success. That's like getting a gym membership and an arsenal of workout clothes and new shoes before you even break a sweat in the gym. If you notice the events that come in and out of your life daily, you'll come to expect that things will change. Don't waste too much time putting your ducks in a row and miss the entire process of your "why".

You wanna be successful? Start answering the questions you ask yourself TODAY! Who do you know that's currently in a place you'd like to be? You can stick to googling things if you want but there's walking talking lessons around you 24/7 if you look hard enough.

If you've got more money and intelligence than your friends or the sum of all your friends it's time to upgrade. If you've maxed out at your job and you're currently experiencing nothing but consistency it's time to move on.

Does your paycheck fluctuate or is it consistent? Often times our work ethic is reflective of our paychecks.. it flatlines. How are you EVER EVER EVER going to do great things in life if you aren't pushed and pulled to do so? Stop sabotaging yourself NOW!

Throw away the alarm clock. Don't let your 9 to 5 wake you up, especially if it's already giving you the Sunday evening blues. Wake up with a purpose not ON purpose. If you're bored with your life's routine do something different to get different results. It doesn't have to be drastic, it's all about baby steps. Stop sleeping through your passions and accepting defeat.

ABOUT THE AUTHOR

After consistently receiving straight F's Terrence quickly learned it's better to cheat than to repeat or so he thought. Giving up and getting comfortable led him to experiencing: repossession, eviction, debt and abandonment. He was once a stranger to hard work and more importantly a stranger to himself.

Until he received the wake up call that would punch him in the face harder than Mike Tyson ever could in his prime. His dad died unexpectedly in his sleep. With remorse, he was suddenly faced with the reality of what happens when you get comfortable and made a decision to live and teach with a purpose.

To schedule your FREE strategy session please visit: YouAreYourOutcome.com

If you would like Terrence Sani to speak at your next corporate event, conference or other setting he can be reached at:

1 (832) 934-4246
Hello@TerrenceSani.com
TerrenceSani.com

Facebook: Facebook.com/terrencesani1
Instagram: @TERRENCESANI

www.ingramcontent.com/pod-product-compliance
Lightning Source LLC
Chambersburg PA
CBHW021407090426
42742CB00009B/1041